Gallery Books
Editor: Peter Fallon

DISSECTING THE HEART

Rosita Boland

DISSECTING THE HEART

Gallery Books

Dissecting the Heart
is first published
simultaneously in paperback
and in a clothbound edition
on 25 April 2003.

The Gallery Press
Loughcrew
Oldcastle
County Meath
Ireland

ISBN 1 85235 343 0 (*paperback*)
    1 85235 344 9 (*clothbound*)

A CIP catalogue record for this book
is available from the British Library.

The Gallery Press acknowledges the financial assistance
of An Chomhairle Ealaíon / The Arts Council, Ireland.

Contents

for Cáitríona
and my other sisters
Judith Murray, Nollaig Ó Fiongháile,
and Selina Guinness

Five Kinds of Water and a Feather

I THE SEA LION'S STOMACH

The sea lion swallowed the pebbles to ballast itself,
like a diver's weightbelt; preventing itself
from coming up to the surface too soon.

A Victorian curiosity, the petrified stomach
is now displayed
under the water-clear surface of a glass case
in an Edinburgh museum.

As we leaned over
we counted two score or more smooth stones
spilling from the split bag

of its too-small stomach.
All the rest of that afternoon I thought
about the sea lion, swallowing its way towards oblivion,
risking too much with every dive.

It is like this between us still, sometimes
misjudging the ballast,
diving clumsily into the uncertain depths

of separate pasts,
distending something vital in the process: let us
always come back to the surface, still breathing,
still buoyant.

2 FLIGHT PATHS

The eighteenth-century Swedish naturalist,
Carolus Linnaeus,
like Aristotle long before him,
was convinced
that swallows wintered underwater
in the riverbeds they nested on.

The truth is no less strange:
small birds flying south to Africa
navigating only by the Pole Star;
a displacement of the elements either way —
like love, when it arrives overnight
and seemingly from nowhere.

Each time we waved the other off
at airports, we had to believe
what was travelling far
would survive to return by instinct
and seem again to have always been there,
swooping and soaring above our joyous heads.

3 RESERVOIR

They drowned a valley in Yorkshire,
near Pately Bridge
forty years ago.
Overnight a village sank from sight

but not from the memories
of those who had lived there.
In the drought of 1995
newspapers ran wire pictures

of a church spire
emerging
from that reservoir.
People who had lived there came back

to stare, to try and remember
the way it had been,
but there are places
one can never return to.

We both thought what we had together
was indestructible, safe-as-houses,
but when the water came flooding in,
nothing was salvaged.

Even if that valley could be drained
and we went back
to look for our damaged home
I fear what we would discover.

Would we ever be able to rebuild it,
or trust we would not waken some night
to hear the water rise once more,
pressing down on us like our past?

4 BEACHING

From Pakistan, scientists announce that they have unearthed a fossil whale with hands, legs, and feet. It is, they are confident, a whale that would have walked on water. — Reuters, 1994

A man once told me
he could feel his leg ghosting beside him
thirty years after its amputation.

Fluent in water, every year
whales flounder on the sands
of coastlines around the world.

It has been like this a long time now.
Far out at sea
something happens. I forget we are

sundered. I move inland.
What instinct tugs me towards
those seductive, fraught sands?

I get beached on the memory of you.
People gather. Push me back
out to sea.

5 SHIPWRECK

We got shipwrecked
on the rocks of each other
and discovered them to be as dangerous
as they were steadfast.

The hoard of our love is lost:
spilled gold that must still
shine on the seabed somewhere;
bright and soft and cold.

6 IMPING

The falconer cast off the hawk,
his raised arm pliant as a branch,
the green fist of his gauntlet
a bud the hawk's wings flowered darkly from.

As it took flight
the bird shed a tail feather.
The falconer retrieved it
and placed it in an inner pocket
with the studied care of one
who presses petals
between the pages of a book.

It was being kept for *imping*.
Should the hawk injure a feather while hunting
the one it had moulted
could be grafted onto what remained.

I had not believed it possible
to repair something that seemed
so irreversibly broken,
to create again
an intact wingspan,
a flight of full potential.

Looking at the Landscape

The sea bursts in over the landscape and takes over.
— Seán McSweeney, Sligo 1996

This landscape of layered oils —
sky, sea, bog, and saltwater fields —
is brimming with surface tension.

Each time I look at this painting
I push off in the same small boat
from the water's edge.

Each time, the waves
remake themselves, spray up
to break anew on the boat's bow

and my eyes become oars
that take me as far out to sea
as I choose to go.

The Last House on the Island

At the last house on the island
they are always losing things.

They lost their washing to the wind
that sent all their linen out to sea.

They lost flowers, hedges, and then trees,
taken yearly by spring tides.

They lost power when the cable snapped
and darkness bloomed within the walls.

They lost their neighbours one by one
who rowed ashore, and did not return.

They lost their bairn to a rogue wave
and then their reason shortly after.

The last house on the island could be a boat
embedded in a shifting shore.

One day soon a storm will launch it
down the slipway of the lawn,

and its twin gables will be taut sails
trimmed for a voyage, shining white.

The Astronaut's Wife

Once you've been to the moon, I don't think there is 'normal'.
— Buzz Aldrin

On our honeymoon
love made us weightless: we orbited
in each other's arms.
We lay in bed
and looked at the moon. We knew
it was illuminating our future.

The day they launched into space
I tracked with awed assurance
the moonlit path from our door to the road.
I thought it led straight to him.

But after they came miraculously back,
after the ticker-tape,
the handshakes, the pictures, the medals,
I slowly realized I had lost him.

Out in the depthless indigo
his mind was still floating
on the Sea of Tranquillity: flotsam
on a tide that never turns.

Now the moon haunts our home.
The blade of its light
slides in through closed shutters.
We wake at night
to see it shining on our skin,
and are afraid to move.

Horizons

i.m. Niamh Nolan, 1968-1999

Horizon
Line at which sea and sky appear to meet.

Like the salmon, you went back
to where you came from: back to Belmullet
where the loose Atlantic and those huge skies pulse
unpredictably against each other.

For ten days you were lost in the horizon,
unreachable
as the place itself. Beyond our ken.

Celestial Horizon
Great circle of the celestial sphere,
plane of which passes through centre of earth.

You were given back to us
out of a celestial horizon.
You had become
a small, bright star-of-the-sea.

On the Horizon
Just imminent, or becoming apparent.

Now we tell your stories for you
and in the uncharted ocean of memory
you glint often, swift
and elusive; light on water.

Lipstick

Home from work one evening
I switched the radio on as usual,
chose a knife and started to slice
red peppers, scallions, wild mushrooms.

I started listening to a programme about Iran.
After the Shah fled, Revolutionary Guards
patrolled the streets of Teheran
looking for stray hairs, exposed ankles
and other signs of female disrespect.

The programme ended.
I was left standing in my kitchen
looking at the chopped vegetables on the table;
the scarlet circles of the peppers
delicate mouths, scattered at random.

When they discovered a woman wearing lipstick
they razor-bladed it off:
replaced one red gash with another.

Diamonds

The Tsarina knew
that some darkness was seeping ever closer.
In the uneasy stillness of their palace
the Romanov women tried to prepare themselves
for whatever lay ahead.

Whispering together one silent dawn, their needles
moving like splinters of light, they ripped open
their silk and whalebone corsets
and secreted diamonds along those many seams.

That same day
Alexandra code-wrote in her diary
'Olga and I arranged our medicines'.
They thought they were ready, prepared
for an uncertain future, their valuables
safely concealed against curve of breast
and hollow of heart.

The Tsarina did not know
they had created a bright filigree
of betrayal: grotesque armour.

Later that year, when the Bolsheviks
came for them at Ipatiev House,
their bullets ricocheted off diamonds.

May Day

for Nollaig

Dreaming on the bus from Galway
this last May Day,
my gaze snagged on doorways near Ballinasloe.

There were knots of yellow gorse
outside scores and scores of doorways
that were blurring past
the windows of the bus.

Someone had been up early
and left them carefully there, the old customs.
Bright burls in the fabric of the day.

I thought of people coming out of their houses
later on in that May Day, of them
lifting the gorse up like torch-flares,
shining the light on their coming year.

Butterflies

In war-zones there are landmines
decorated with butterflies
and left on the grassy pathways
of rural villages.

The children come
down the familiar lanes and fields.
Hands outstretched, they reach triumphant
for these bright, elusive insects —
themselves becoming wingèd in the act,
gaudy and ephemeral.

Sightless

1

The child's first memory
was of standing in an open doorway
listening to her mother
singing a song about a bird flying.
She wondered what it was,
and what flight was.

Since then, she had held a bird
in the egg of her cupped hands,
its wings fluttering against
the membrane of her shocked fingers.

For her, flight now means
that sudden, astonishing absence,
conjured up when her hands broke open
and the bird disappeared
into the beyond.

2

She drew pictures
of what she thought her world looked like.
'This one has hills in it.
And my house.'

Vertical lines marched across the page; her hills.
Among them, a small square box
drawn tight and snug as a safe.

In it, one dot of a door,
round as a keyhole to her world.

My Mother's Winter Coat

Reluctant to throw them out,
for years my mother
squirrelled away her old clothes
in hiding places around the house.
Then I discovered them.

Now I wear her cotton dresses
printed with roses; the linen suits
cut in '50s style;
and, my favourite, her black cashmere
winter coat.

Each year I have it dry-cleaned,
sew the buttons on again
and tighten the thread of the hem,
choosing to ignore those places
where the seams are starting to split
and the satin lining is fraying.

Last year my mother told me
she bought that coat to wear
the winter she was carrying me.

Every sharp morning since then
I've drawn the coat around me
and leaned into the wind
with a new awareness of the future:
just as my mother must have done
that year, when this coat
contained our shared outline.

Six Museums

WHITE — CUPID AND PSYCHE

Nineteen in Paris, and everything new;
a week that opened like a vista
and let me see the horizon.

In the Louvre
I stood for half an hour beside
Canova's sculpture of Cupid and Psyche
and felt the sensation of some discovery
beating through my blood.

The noonday sun
shone through Cupid's carved wings
making them translucent,
as if something was stirring
within the white marble.

I saw the pure oblivion of their unity, made evident
by the tenderness with which Cupid held
his trustful sleeping Psyche;
their entwined arms a circle
through which love eternally looped.

Years later, lying beside the man I loved,
I saw folds of sunlight on his back,
remembered with joy those white wings.

GOLD — THE GLENINSHEEN GORGET

for Martin Cowley

The glass case in the National Museum
can hardly contain the extravagance of it.
That handspan of gold around the neck,
a hammered perfection
of collar and decorated disc,
stitched together with twisted gold wire.
Gorget: a piece of armour for the throat.

It was found in 1932, glinting
in a fissure of the Burren, glimpsed there
by an astonished farmer going about his business.
The folded collar in the crevice
had been concealed
for a millennium and more:
secret fusion of stone and gold.

To look at this gorget is to realize
that discoveries are always possible,
that a life can be transmuted
by the alchemy of chance.
This has become my own armour.
It winks and gleams
somewhere within.

SIENNA — A PIECE OF *Skylab*

In the Esperance Town Museum, Western Australia,
there were the usual relics
from the pioneering days;
meat-safes, gold-mining certificates,
and old boots.
The wooden cabinets also held
moths, butterflies,
and shells of astonishing colours.

Everything was slightly dusty, slightly subdued.
The two ladies at the entrance desk
fanned themselves and spoke in low voices.

I stumbled over something on the floor
that looked like a rusty old bath,
sienna-coloured, and contorted.
Neatly printed on the faded card
were these words: 'A piece of *Skylab*
which, after six years,
broke up in space
and fell to earth, 11 July 1979,
scattering into the Indian Ocean
and the outlying territory of Esperance.'

The corroded metal beneath my hand
transformed
into the fragmented chrysalis
of flight.

BROWN — THE HAIR HURLING BALL

They were made by young women
and those who were just-married
as love-tokens for their men,
from the fifteenth century
until the mid-nineteenth.

This one in Collins Barracks
was found in Munster.
Brown hair of cow and horse
carefully plaited and woven with love and hope
into the intricate interlace
of a perfect sphere.

My hand is extended, palm up,
trying to guess what the clasp of it
would feel like, when I realize
I must be repeating the gesture
of the woman who made it:
how, when it was finished, she must have held it,
tightening her hand over possibilities.

BLUE — THE PORTLAND VASE

It looks black.
Black as a starless night.
And then, slowly, I see a change:
a marvellous inky-blueness
glowing in the glass, infused there
like the colour of that transition
from darkness to first light.

In 1845 William Mulcahy smashed it.
Imagine the scene in the British Museum:
the two-thousand-year-old roar of sundering glass
and the Portland Vase suddenly becoming unmade
in a strange conjuring trick, magicked instantly
into hundreds of tiny pieces;
fragments, splinters, and shards.

Yet there it still is today. Reassembled
with patience, skill, and glue.
Looking at the vase,
I can't stop wondering where things begin
and end, or if there is only continuance:
in the way that day deepens into night; some penumbra
where light and shade meet, and become one.

BRONZE — THE HORSE AND LITTLE JOCKEY OF ARTEMISION

The horse was the first to emerge from the sea;
a powerful, spirited Poseidon
rearing up from the turquoise Grecian waters.

Later, the shipwreck at Cape Artemision
yielded another ancient bronze;
an ephebe-jockey,

absurdly smaller than the horse
the curators of Athens' Archaeological Museum
eventually matched him with.

Yet they look strangely right,
the flying-hooved horse, taking an unseen obstacle,
urged on by the little jockey:

as unlikely a pair as you and I,
all of us salvage, now journeying as one,
leaping into the bright unknown
and taking our chances together.

Dissecting the Heart

Unfortunately people don't tend to donate hearts. They have romantic associations.
— Maurice Neligan, *Morning Ireland*, 2001

1

We could blame centuries of literature;
men and women losing their hearts
to each other.
Or blame the pinked edges of Victorian Valentines
with their copperplate confessions,
Dear heart, dearest love.

2

Vesalius wanted to dissect
the elusive secrets of the heart.
In Padua the magistrates obliged.
The gallows swung
just before Anatomy lessons.

Knives whet,
he awaited delivery of each cadaver
with the eagerness of a lover
impatient to solve all mysteries
in the one he desires.

It was William Harvey
who discovered the heart
was the precious centre of the body:
cushioned like a jewel in a container of muscle,
vital in its function of circulating blood.

3

There is no drawing of a soul
nor an anatomical image of love.
The heart has become the definable tissue
that stands for the indefinable:
for what makes us quicken and enliven,
for what pulses through us and between us.

Teeth

Unlikely jewels,
the modern language of dentistry
hints at teeth's odd value, their strange history.
Porcelain. Pearl-white.
Crowns. Gold.

The first set falls out. Milk teeth,
the assigned colour of innocence,
left like a fable
at night under a child's pillow
in exchange for a coin.

Three hundred years ago
it was the practice to pay a small fee
for pulling teeth from the poor.
They were set in ivory gums for nobility;
the first false teeth.

Some eighteenth-century sets were ornamental,
made of silver, or mother-of-pearl.
Lord John Hervey of England commissioned a set
in Italian agate, and startled courtiers
with an eerie, translucent smile.

Later, teeth were extracted from the fallen
of the American Civil War and shipped
to Europe for re-use by the wealthy.
They chewed on meat and tobacco
with the aid of dead soldiers.

Later still, gold teeth
were plundered from the mouths of those
who died in the chambers
of Auschwitz and other camps,
and melted into jewellery.

There must have been men and women
who went on to wear those circles of tainted gold
on their wedding days:
the rings like open shining jaws
waiting for a chance to bite.

Fontanelle

for Jasmine, Molly, Doran, and Phoebe

It's such a disquieting gap
where the membrane dips
over the parietal bones.

Delicate and dangerous:
the thinnest ice on the deepest lake,
the snowy crevasse in the glacier,

the open well concealed by brambles.
My instinct is to seal it
to stop your soul escaping.

But I must watch instead,
must wait until time unaided
completes what's already been begun,

must wait for that bittersweet surprise
of realizing one day how-you've-grown
and are moving headlong through the world.

The First X-ray

Experimenting alone in his laboratory,
Wilhelm Röntgen pulled the curtains
to seal in the darkness.
Expecting fluorescence,
he prepared. Induction coil.
Electrodes. Glass tube.

Black cardboard.
A chance scrap of paper became both
mystery and clue. It shone.
He discovered X-rays that night,
became an archaeologist of light,
an archivist of what lies beneath.

There was public shock in seeing bodies
newly translated by science:
many who saw his photographs
of skeletal bones and organs
also saw their skin transformed to shroud
and mortality in the shape of a skull.

The first X-ray Wilhelm Röntgen took
was of his wife's hand.
The photograph survives.
Her splayed fingers
are outstretched in a gesture
that reaches like a handshake

across three centuries.
Anna Röntgen's wedding ring
has come up solid
against the shadow of those small bones:
a love-knot
time has not unfastened.

The Brain

I HOLES

For centuries it was believed
that the mind and memory were located
in holes of the brain,
secreted like some mysterious creatures
within the brain's ventricles,
too shy to be coaxed out;
never sighted.

2 PHRENOLOGY

Like some Renaissance Cabinet of Curiosities,
Franz Josef Gall divided the head into
twenty-seven parts.

Porcelain models of the cranium
illustrated his theory of phrenology.
Lines defined specific areas of
Imitation, Wonder, Cruelty,
Wit, Secretiveness, Humour,
Benevolence, Self-esteem, Hope,
and all the other random elements
of what he thought
made a human tick.

People held their heads in their hands
trying to discover what was inside
and who they were.
They traced fingers over
the landscape of their skulls,
searching for clues about themselves
in the lumps and bumps that lay beneath.

3   CHARLES BABBAGE'S BRAIN

When the mathematical genius died
his brain was removed,
split in half,
studied, and preserved
in London's Royal College of Surgeons.

A male brain
is the size of two fists,
weighs three pounds,
and contains approximately
twenty-eight billion nerve cells:
a fantastic tool, containing the same endless
permutations of possibilities
as the calculating machine
invented by Babbage in 1833;
the first computer.

Charles Babbage's brain
is still on public display.
It has become part fetish, part medical history
and part something else:
a fascination with what his brain created
and what it represents now;
some husk-like object
akin perhaps to an empty matchbox, except
that the fires ignited
by those spent matches
are still casting a magnificent lambency.

Breath

Forensic scientists have identified criminals
by the imprint of an ear on a door,
tracking their DNA by traces of sweat.

We literally exude life, cannot help
but leave our marks behind
on surfaces composed both of matter and of mind
as clearly as if scratched
by a diamond on a piece of glass.

The dead must also leave behind
more than we know: some secretion
concealed in the space
once occupied by lives; where the atmosphere
pulled into shapes around them,
where contact was made with time and place
and which registered there
like the breath that spreads clarity
across a frozen windowpane.

Fingerprints

The body changes
but the pattern of fingerprints
stays constant over a lifetime.

A matching set of prints
has never been discovered
between those whose prints are recorded.

We can only trust that it is true,
hope in the whorls, loops, and ovals
that tighten inside each other
like Chinese boxes,
the last unopened one which is believed
to contain uniqueness.

Hair

One of the few relics of the dead
permitted by Western society.
Victorian rings, lockets, and brooches
containing snips of twisted hair
displayed between Whitby jet and thin glass
were worn both as
a formal statement of mourning
and as the final keepsake
of belovèd men, women, and children.

More than a century on
antique shops sell Victorian hair jewellery
as quaintly eerie curios of their period.

Whitby is mined out,
so the focus now is on the jet
while the hair seems meaningless,
stranded somewhere between
a newly-prized black lignite
and a brittle transparency:
a *memento mori* that has forgotten
both those whose memory it once evoked
and those who wore it to remember them by.

Tears

The Pharaohs
respected their tear-shedding eyes so much
they had a different doctor for each one.

The Greeks and Romans kept their tears.
Some ancient tear bottles survive;
slender, wide-lipped, with a rounded end
and made of iridescent glass.

Into these, mourners wept their sorrow
and their memories of the newly-dead.
The bottles were buried with the bodies:

little glimmers of grief and love
welling up underground;
prismatic compasses, ready for a reading
of whatever lay ahead.